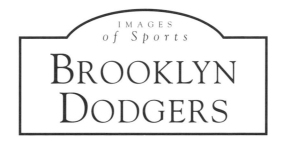

IMAGES
of Sports

BROOKLYN
DODGERS

Over the years, the Brooklyn Dodgers experienced the ups and downs of any major-league franchise. They celebrated long and short winning streaks and weathered storms of all kinds, but fans always stuck with them—even during the travails of World War II. In this 1943 view, first baseman Howie Schultz (left) poses with bullpen catcher Joe Sosovic for a study in contrasts.

IMAGES
of Sports

BROOKLYN
DODGERS

Mark Rucker

ARCADIA

First printed in 2002.

Published by Arcadia Publishing,
an imprint of Tempus Publishing, Inc.
2A Cumberland Street
Charleston, SC 29401

Printed in Great Britain.

Library of Congress Catalog Card Number: 2001099625

For all general information contact Arcadia Publishing at:
Telephone 843-853-2070
Fax 843-853-0044
E-Mail sales@arcadiapublishing.com

For customer service and orders:
Toll-Free 1-888-313-2665

Visit us on the internet at http://www.arcadiapublishing.com

*This book is dedicated to George Lowis, who spent an important
part of his youth at Ebbets Field. His mother would send him off every
Saturday with a sack lunch to watch the Dodgers, and he remembers it all.*

In the 1860s, many of the teams that competed for the annual national championship came from Brooklyn and Manhattan. The interborough rivalry developed with the game's rapid growth. Fans, or "cranks," actively followed their teams, and newspapers followed the fans. In this 1865 woodcut from *Frank Leslie's Weekly*, a catcher from the New York Mutuals puts out an Atlantic batter on a foul tip.

Author's note: All images are courtesy of Transcendental Graphics unless otherwise noted.

CONTENTS

BIBLIOGRAPHY

Chadwick, Henry, ed. *Spalding's Official Baseball Guide*. New York: American Sports Publishing Company, 1889, 1892, 1896, and 1899.

Clark, Dick, and Larry Lester. *The Negro Leagues Book*. Cleveland, Ohio: Society for American Baseball Research, 1994.

Cohen, Neft, Johnson, and Deutsch. *The World Series*. New York: Dial Press, 1976.

Graham, Frank. *The Brooklyn Dodgers*. New York: Putnam, 1947.

Lowry, Philip. *Green Cathedrals*. Cleveland, Ohio: Society for American Baseball Research, 1996.

Okkonen, Marc. *Baseball Uniforms of the 20th Century*. New York: Sterling, 1991.

Peverelley, Charles. *Book of American Pastimes*. New York: American News Company, 1868.

Porter, David, ed. *Biographical Dictionary of American Sports*. New York: Greenwood Press, 1987.

Reichler, Joe. *Great All-Time Baseball Record Book*. New York: MacMillan, 1981.

Riley, James. *The Biographical Encyclopedia of the Negro Baseball Leagues*. New York: Carroll & Graf, 1994.

Shatzkin, Mike. *The Ballplayers*. New York: Arbor House, 1990.

Thompson, S.C. *All-Time Rosters of Major League Baseball Clubs*. New York: A.S. Barnes, 1967.

Thorn, John, and Pete Palmer. *Total Baseball*. New York: Warner Books, 1991.

The pennant-winning 1952 Dodger season was an excellent one for fans in Brooklyn. Seven of the team's most popular starters are pictured on the dugout steps. They are, from left to right, Carl Furillo, Jackie Robinson, Roy Campanella, Pee Wee Reese, Duke Snider, Andy Pafko, and Gil Hodges.

INTRODUCTION

Bounded by the Atlantic, New York Harbor, the East River, and Queens, the 73-square-mile borough of Brooklyn always offered lots of room to play baseball. In the earliest days, the two prominent Brooklyn ballparks were the Capitoline Grounds and the Union Grounds. The Capitoline Grounds, located in the Brownsville section of the Bedford-Stuyvesant neighborhood, was built by Reuben Decker in 1862 on a farmer's field. Many important contests between the finest teams in America were witnessed there at the corner of Putnam and Nostrand Avenues. In the Williamsburgh section, the Union Grounds was situated at the junction of Lee and Marcy Avenues. The park, previously a large ice rink for the use of the Union Skating Club, was in continuous use for professional ball until 1877.

Washington Park, located in the Red Hook section, experienced a number of incarnations. First opened in 1883 for minor-league play, the field lay near the Gowanus Canal and the Bay Ridge railroad tracks. The American Association Trolley Dodgers claimed Washington Park as home from 1884 to 1889. After falling into disrepair, Washington Park was reborn diagonally across the street from its old location. It opened in 1898 and remained the Dodgers' ballpark until the end of 1912. For a brief period in the late 1880s, Brooklyn's American Association representatives used Ridgewood Park, constructed at the Queens-Brooklyn border between Myrtle and Wyckoff Avenues and Weirfield and Decatur Streets.

Washington Park closed for a good reason. Dodger owner Charlie Ebbets had reorganized the Dodgers and oversaw the construction of a brand-new stadium in a part of Flatbush that had been known as Pigtown. Ebbets Field opened on April 9, 1913, and was the happy home of Dodger teams and fans until the ignominious departure of the Dodgers at the close of the 1957 season. Left field was bordered by Montgomery Street, and right field by Bedford Avenue. The third-base line was next to McKeever Place, and the first-base line was next to Sullivan Place.

These sites attracted sports enthusiasts from all over the New York area. In the beginning, many simply wanted to see the new game of baseball that was sweeping the city. Soon, crowds grew with an influx of curiosity seekers, gamblers, and club members cheering their first nines. The ballpark was the center of social activity in Brooklyn on game day. As baseball became entrenched as the national pastime, Brooklyn's teams acquired national followings, with large crowds at every important contest. Revenue began to flow from gate receipts as professional leagues delivered top-notch talent to larger ballparks with larger capacities. Right from the start, the borough was crazy for its baseball and wild about its teams.

Brooklyn developed in the shadow of Manhattan, which always treated its neighbor with disdain. The butt of jokes from New York City's earliest days, Brooklyn citizens could not only endure the ridicule but could come up with funnier versions about themselves. Baseball success became a symbol of pride for Brooklyn's citizens and was a means to best their rivals across the East River. When the Excelsiors whipped the Knickerbockers of New York, or the Atlantics beat the Gothams, there was cause for great rejoicing.

In the 20th century, Brooklyn continued to grow in both population and baseball prominence. If separated from New York City, Brooklyn would have stood as America's third largest city. The fan base was huge, and its loyalty was unquestionable.

The Trolley Dodgers of the 1890s began winning pennants as the new century began. Every year, the fans would hope for a winner, but loyalty more than anything else distinguished

Brooklyn rooters. The team could finish third, fourth, or sixth and the fans would still come out. A first-place finish, which occurred often enough for World Series appearances in almost every decade, sent the crowds into delirious ecstasy. The National League pennants were not gathered in bunches until the end of the 1940s. Before that, the Dodgers won in 1890, 1899, 1900, 1916, 1920, and 1941. Additionally, they picked up flags in 1947, 1949, 1952, 1953, 1955, and 1956. Frustration set in with one World Series defeat after another at the hands of the New York Yankees in the late 1940s and early 1950s. That was all set right in the 1955 World Series, when the Bums (as the Dodgers were affectionately called) finally got over. Win or lose, Ebbets Field was always full of supporters.

Perhaps it was the long-suffering, never-say-die attitude in Brooklyn that made the loss of the club so difficult. No other city, other than perhaps St. Louis, had given as much to their baseball team as had the citizens of Brooklyn. In the 1950s, owner Walter O'Malley could claim to have the loudest, funniest, and most dedicated fans in the United States. He made money from gate receipts, advertising, and concessions in amounts that made other owners jealous. Yet the money, the exuberance, and the fan loyalty were not enough for him. Secretly making agreements with New York Giants owner Horace Stoneham, O'Malley arranged for the franchise to move to Los Angeles for the 1958 season, while the Giants went to San Francisco. The two owners saw greener pastures on the other side of the country, but New York fans saw red. For the borough of Brooklyn, this was inconceivable. The mayor of New York, the borough president, the city council, and citizens groups all fought the move. Although it seemed like the removal of a vital organ from the city, O'Malley and Stoneham were in control. Dodger fans in Brooklyn would never forget. Sadness and anger settled over the city, but wonderful memories had been generated through the years. Many of those fond memories will be reviewed in these pages.

One
1850–1879

The Excelsior club was formed in 1854 by a group of athletic, middle-class Brooklyn residents dedicated to America's new game. They played a "gentlemanly" game, but in a fast and lively style with victory in mind. In 1860, the club organized the first-ever tour, which helped introduce the young game to crowds in central and western New York cities. Starting on July 2, 1860, the Excelsiors met the competition in Albany, defeating the Champion club. In Troy, they beat the Victory club and, in Rochester, bested both the Live Oak and Flour City clubs. They beat the Niagaras in Buffalo and topped the Hudson River club in Newburgh. Dominating every contest, the Excelsiors brought a new form of entertainment to thousands upstate. The team's stars, including catcher Jim Leggett and pitcher Jim Creighton, were soon known to all ballplayers in the country. Asa Brainard, their right fielder, was to become the pitcher for the first avowedly professional team, the Cincinnati Red Stockings. Pictured are the Excelsiors of 1860. They are, from left to right, T. Reynolds, J.C. Whiting, J. Creighton, H.B. Polhemus, A.T. Pearsall, E. Russell, J.R. Leggett, A. Brainard, and G. Flanley.

JAMES CREIGHTON,

In 1862, Jim Creighton died after a cricket match, probably from a ruptured spleen or hernia. Creighton had developed a fastball with a wrist snap, revolutionizing pitching. His delivery was controversial but legal. He was beloved by all in the baseball community and became the sport's first martyr. This photographic trade card, issued by the Peck and Snyder Sporting Goods Company, eulogized him on the reverse.

Formed originally from the stevedores, longshoremen, and other Brooklyn dockworkers, the Atlantic club developed a new and aggressive style of play. This blue-collar team loved to beat up on the gentleman's clubs, such as the Excelsiors. This 1860 *carte de visite* photograph is the earliest-known image of the club. The Atlantics had a long and glorious run, becoming the preeminent club in the New York area.

New York City was a hotbed of baseball activity in the 1860s, as illustrated in this woodcut from an 1865 issue of *Frank Leslie's Weekly*. Three years after his death, Jim Creighton was still center stage (his bust shrouded at the top center). The image is framed with representative players from each major team in the area. Standing up for the Brooklyn clubs are Joe Leggett for the Excelsiors, Pete O'Brien for the Atlantics, Mort Rogers for the Resolutes, John Grum for the Eckfords, S.G. Leland for the Enterprise, Robert Manly for the Stars, and Thomas Dakin for the Putnams. The central scene shows a game in progress at the Union Grounds between rival Brooklyn nines, the Eckfords and Atlantics. The Union Grounds, one of the most popular sites for ball play in the city, hosted many key championship games.

The Resolute club included pitcher Mort Rogers, shown sitting in the center (holding a ball) in this 1861 photograph. After moving to Boston, Rogers published a baseball newspaper and series of photographic score cards. His brother A.H. Rogers (standing in a top hat on the far left) became the secretary for the National Association of Base Ball Players. A young Henry Chadwick, the father of baseball journalism, stands on the far right.

Critical championship battles in the mid-1860s often involved the Atlantics and the Philadelphia Athletics. They played alternately in Brooklyn and Philadelphia, with the Atlantics on top most of the time. They would play each other two to four times a season, occasions that would bring out sportsmen, fanatics, hustlers, and gamblers in droves. The

Rivalries like the one between the Philadelphia Athletics and the Brooklyn Atlantics in the 1860s always brought notice. The national championship could often come down to a final battle between these two. In 1866, a *Harper's Weekly* artist compared the nines by placing line-ups one behind the other. They look pretty evenly matched.

Atlantics were their hometown boys. They represented a consistency, a strong work ethic, and an intelligence that suited the fans in Brooklyn. They put Brooklyn on the baseball map year after year and were always entertaining. This 1865 panoramic woodcut from *Harper's Weekly* shows the Atlantics playing the Athletics in Philadelphia.

In his classic mid-19th-century book, Charles Peverelley wrote that the Atlantic club "was organized August 14, 1855, and from the day of its entrance upon the base ball field it has occupied and filled a front-rank position as a crack playing club. Unlike many of its kindred associations, who place a strong nine in the field for one summer, and perhaps a weak body of players for the ensuing season, the Atlantics have always and at all times had a nine from whom any club might almost despair of winning any lasting laurels. It is this extraordinary and unvarying success, which has gained for them the title of 'Champion.'" The team was honored in 1865 with this full-page woodcut in *Harper's Weekly*.

Thos P Pratt. Sid C Smith. R B Pearce. Jos Start. Chas J Smith. John C Chapman. F B Crane. Frank Norton.
PITCHER. RIGHT FIELD. SHORT STOP. FIRST BASE. THIRD BASE. LEFT FIELD. SECOND BASE. CATCHER.
Peter O'Brien. John Galvin.
Mgr. CENTRE FIELD.

LATER PLAYERS OF CLUB
THAN 1865.
Lipman Pike,
Jas McDonald,
Geo. Hall.

Atlantic Base Ball Club
OF BROOKLYN
Champions of America. 1864, 1865, 1866, 1868 and 1870.

LATER PLAYERS OF CLUB
THAN 1865.
Robert Ferguson.
Chas Mills
Geo. Zettlein

The Atlantics were so good that they claimed the national championship five different years in the 1860s, starting in 1864. This large presentation photograph with a calligraphic mount was likely made for the Atlantics' clubhouse. It celebrates the team's history and lists the names of its most preeminent nine. Dickey Pearce (third from the left) has been credited with developing the bunt, as well as strategy for shortstops. Joe "Old Reliable" Start played a 25-year career, starting in 1861. He starred for the Atlantics from 1861 to 1870, while third baseman Charlie Smith was named the best ballplayer in America more than once. Pete O'Brien (bearded in the suit) was an Atlantic senior by 1870. He had led the team in the 1850s and early 1860s. John "Death to Flying Things" Chapman was nicknamed for his fielding prowess. After his playing career, he became a manager, leading the Louisville club to a pennant in 1890. (Courtesy National Baseball Library, Cooperstown, New York.)

Everybody loves a winner, and that includes advertisers. The Peck and Snyder Sporting Goods Company continued to issue photographic trade cards, as they did for Jim Creighton. Here, they commemorate the champions of 1868 in a photographic promotional piece. The new faces on the team were George Zettlein (pitcher) and Bob Ferguson, both of whom had long and celebrated careers in the game.

By the time this Atlantics team was playing in the professional National Association in 1873, they were a weakened version of the nines from the 1860s. This 1873 squad won 22 and lost 33, finishing sixth in a field of eight. The following year, when they finished with an unbelievable 2-42 record, was the last for a professional team to represent Brooklyn until 1884.

16

Candy Cumming is said to be the inventor of the curve ball. True or not, he is a member of the National Baseball Hall of Fame. In this lovely tintype, he is standing to the left of an unidentified teammate, both members of the Star of Brooklyn club. Cummings became a Star in 1869 and hurled for them in the subsequent two seasons.

Cummings earned the pitcher-of-the-year honor from Henry Chadwick in 1871. He then joined the National Association, winning 33, 33, and 28 between 1872 and 1874 for three different teams. He moved to Hartford in 1875 and signed with Hartford's National League entry in 1876. However, the franchise suffered and, for financial reasons, moved to Brooklyn for the last half of the season.

In the winter of 1867, a series of baseball games on ice was scheduled, this one in Washington Park, Brooklyn. The idea did not catch on, but a permanent rule change grew out of these experiments. After these contests, the batter was allowed to run past first base on a ball hit to the infield.

Brooklyn did have teams of a local character, as well as national powers. Here, a player for the Montana club poses in a photographer's elaborately decorated studio. This club operated in the mid-1870s in a little-known section of Brooklyn, near what is now the border with the borough of Queens.

Two
1880–1899

Brooklyn jumped back into the big leagues, the American Association, in 1884 and considerably livened up Washington Park in the Red Hook section. Since difficulties and adventures in getting to the park were common, the team got the nickname "Trolley Dodgers." In 1884, they finished with a 40-64 record, 9th in a field of 13. Improvement continued through the decade until the team posted a mark of 88-52 in 1888, followed by a pennant in 1889, when the group shown here won 93 and lost 44. They are, from left to right, as follows: (front row) Mike Hughes; (middle row) George Pinckney, Bob Caruthers, Hub Collins, manager Bill McGunnigle, Oyster Burns, Bob Clark, and Tommy Lovett; (back row) Germany Smith, Pop Corkhill, Adonis Terry, Dave Foutz, Darby O'Brien, Doc Bushong, and Joe Visner.

This photograph, looking from right-center field from atop a small hill, was taken on Decoration Day at Washington Park. The St. Louis Browns were playing the Trolley Dodgers on this lovely field, which was bordered by Fourth and Fifth Avenues and Third and Fifth Streets in Red Hook. It was a vacation day for Americans, and the ball fans of Brooklyn were counted in the thousands. The Browns, led by Charlie Comiskey, had won championships in the two preceding seasons in the American Association, and the hometown boys had been

playing them tough. This remarkable view shows what appears to be a throw home from the center fielder, with the runner on third breaking for the plate. An enormous Brooklyn Furniture Company advertisement sits atop the bleacher fence, and the grandstand complex looks like an architectural conglomerate. Everyone is in their Sunday best, Old Glory paints the breeze above the grandstand, and the national pastime is alive and well.

Clarke.
Burdock.
Bushong.
Pinkney.

5. Peeples.
6. Smith.
7. Foutz.

8. O'Brien.
9. Caruthers.
10. Orr.

11. Rad
12. Ter
13. Hug
14. McC

BROOKYN BALL CLUB, 1888.

The Brooklyn photographer Joseph Hall, whose studios were host to major-league ballplayers from all over the country, plied his trade also in Washington Park, as he did for this portrait of the 1888 team. In the prosperous days of the late 1880s, Hall's photography was purchased by tobacconists for promotions and printed in enormous sizes for presentation photographs. His work is now prized by historians and collectors alike. The pitchers for Brooklyn's second-place crew had a good year, with Adonis Terry (sixth from left, front row) at 13-8, Mike Hughes (seventh from left, front row) at 25-13, Dave Foutz (fourth from left, back row) at 12-7, and Bob Caruthers (fifth from left, back row) at 29-15. When Caruthers was not pitching, he was playing the outfield, logging 51 games in the garden in the 1888 season.

The art of the scorecard had become well developed by the time these samples were produced for Dodger games in 1887. The example to the right features a portrait of starting infielder George Pinckney, who played second base, shortstop, and third base for Brooklyn teams from 1885 to 1891. He was a sharp fielder and decent hitter who led the league in walks in 1886 with 70. In 1888, he led the league in runs with 134. William "Adonis" Terry adorns the scorecard below. He was a fan favorite, especially with the ladies. Terry pitched for Brooklyn from 1884 to 1891 and won 20 games three times for the club. His best season was 1890, when he earned 26 victories as a National Leaguer.

Dave Orr was one of the sluggers of the mid-1880s. The first baseman batted .305 for Brooklyn but played for them only in 1888. He had impressed many with his 21 triples in 1885 and 31 triples in 1886, but his total was down to five in 1888, and it appeared Orr had lost his speed.

Dave "Scissors" Foutz was a versatile athlete who played two years for Brooklyn's American Association team. He spent his last seven seasons with the borough's National League franchise. Foutz played the field and pitched, but Brooklyn acquired him from St. Louis mainly for his hitting and fielding skills. In his years with Brooklyn, he won only 33 games. However, playing first base and outfield, he steadily drove in and scored runs.

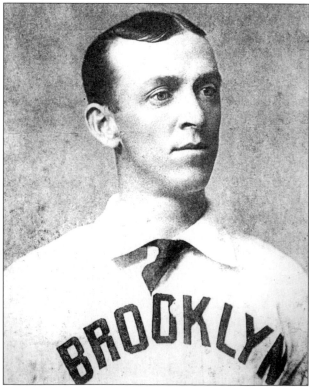

"Parisian" Bob Caruthers spent only one winter visiting France, but that was enough to give him the nickname for life. He was a complete ballplayer. He pitched, winning a total of 218 games in the bigs. He also played outfield and hit, recording a career average of .282. He toiled for Brooklyn from 1888 to 1891.

Thomas P. "Oyster" Burns had an 11-year major-league career and a lifetime batting average of .300. He came to Brooklyn in 1889, helping the American Association team win a pennant. He stayed on to finish his career in the city in 1895. He mostly played outfield for the Dodgers, with his high point being 1890, when he scored 102 runs and knocked in 128.

Dave Foutz appears again in one of a group of remarkable action photographs published in 1889 in *Frank Leslie's Weekly*. We get a sense of Foutz's height as he follows through on a pitch in a Washington Park warm-up. By 19th-century standards, his six-foot-two-inch frame was towering.

If Mike Griffin had played a full career, he would have been a Hall of Famer. He retired at age 33, among the finest outfielders in the game. His last eight years were spent in Brooklyn, where he batted over .300 five times. He was also very fast, compiling 264 stolen bases as a Dodger and averaging over 100 runs scored per year.

John Montgomery Ward may well have been the smartest of all ballplayers in the 1800s. He was an athlete of the highest quality, but he was also a lawyer and a labor organizer. Ward was the moving force behind the Players' League, which lasted only one year: 1890. Obviously a leader, he managed Brooklyn's entry in "the Brotherhood" (as the Players' League was called) and brought them to a second-place finish. He then took over Brooklyn's National League team for 1891 and 1892. In 1891, the club finished sixth, but Ward whipped the Dodgers into shape for the 1892 season, when they won 95 and lost 59, a record that would have won them a championship in other years. In this case, the result was third. Ward served as a manager and played shortstop and second base. He led the league in stolen bases in 1892 with 88.

The 1895 version of the Brooklyn Dodgers finished in a tie for fifth in a large National League field. There were, however, some bright spots, as Bill "Brickyard" Kennedy won 19 games. Pictured from left to right are the following: (front row) Ed Stein, Tommy Corcoran, and Brickyard Kennedy; (middle row) Henry Hines, Buster Burrell, Ad Gumbert, Bert Abbey, George Treadway, Billy Shindle, Tom Daly, Dan Daub, and George Schoch; (back row) Joe Mulvey, Con Dailey, Candy LaChance, Dave Foutz, Mike Griffin, Jack Grim, John Anderson, and Tommy Burns.

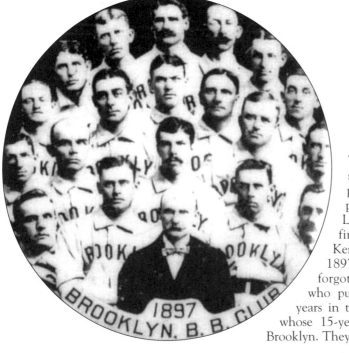

This bit of memorabilia is a souvenir from 1897. The photographic collage of player portraits includes Candy LaChance, the hard-hitting first baseman; Brickyard Kennedy, who won 18 games in 1897; John Anderson, a now-forgotten journeyman outfielder who put up steady numbers for 14 years in the league; and Fielder Jones, whose 15-year career began in 1896 in Brooklyn. They finished only sixth in 1897.

After the 1898 season, manager Ned Hanlon jumped from Baltimore to Brooklyn, bringing the core of his team with him. At the same time, a popular theater piece running in the area was called *Hanlon's Superbas,* resulting in a new nickname for the team. For the next 15 years, Brooklyn's ballplayers were known as the Superbas.

Ed Stein played only eight years in the majors, and six of them were in a Brooklyn uniform. Stein and Brickyard Kennedy were the muscle of the pitching staff from 1892 to 1895. Stein won 27 games twice for the Dodgers, in 1892 and 1894. He won 19 games in 1893 and 15 games in 1895. In all, Stein recorded 91 wins in Brooklyn, but third place was the best the team did while he was on the roster.

All four of these Baltimore Orioles are deservedly members of the National Baseball Hall of Fame. After the 1898 season, three of them moved from Maryland to the Brooklyn club with Ned Hanlon, their manager. "Wee" Willie Keeler (left, back row) was a clever batsman remembered for his quip "Keep your eye on the ball, and hit 'em where they ain't." Seated beneath him is Joe Kelley, the reliable .300 hitter, base stealer, and all-around good glove man. Sitting to the right is Hughie "Ee-Yah" Jennings. Known more from his later days as a manager, Jennings put together 12 solid major-league seasons as a shortstop. Only John McGraw (right, back row) stayed in Baltimore to lead the Orioles through their last big-league season until 1957. It must have been particularly galling for McGraw to see his compatriots win 88 games and the pennant in 1899, while his gutsy .390 batting average could only help the Orioles to a fourth-place finish.

Three

1900–1909

This team, the 1898 Orioles of Baltimore, formed the core of the 1900 National League champion Brooklyn Superbas. In addition to Willie Keeler, Hughie Jennings, and Joe Kelley, Brooklyn got Jim Hughes (standing, far right) and Dan McGann (sitting, third from right). The players received from the Orioles revitalized baseball in Brooklyn, which had seen finishes no higher than fifth since 1892. The fresh, fast, and crafty crew inspired a new following at Washington Park. The 1899 Superbas were stronger than the 1900 incarnation, but not by much. In 1900, they won 82 games to gain the flag, six fewer than the year before. They played Jennings at first, Tom Daly at second, Lave Cross at third, and Bill Dahlen at shortstop in 1900. In the outfield were Willie Keeler, Joe Kelley, and Fielder Jones. Duke Farrell and Deacon McGuire were behind the plate. Joseph "Iron Man" McGinnity, Brickyard Kennedy, and Frank Kitson were their front-line pitchers.

Joseph McGinnity spent only one year in a Brooklyn uniform before moving to the Giants across the river. However, his 28 wins led the league and made the difference in the team's 1900 season. McGinnity started 44 games that year (a little less than a third of the total played that season) and also led the National League in winning percentage and innings pitched. He would be missed. (Courtesy Carnegie Library, Pittsburgh.)

Hughie Jennings and his cohorts played at a time when photographs on the field were seldom taken. We are lucky to have a number of valuable photographs of Brooklyn's top players when they kicked off the 20th century by bringing a pennant home. In that victorious year, Jennings played shortstop and second base but mostly first base.

Willie Keeler stood five feet four inches tall and weighed in at about 140 pounds. His speed was famous, and he developed the "Baltimore chop" while with the Orioles. The technique involved hitting down on the pitch, causing the ball to bounce high enough off the dirt to allow the batter to cross first base before the throw. His 44-game hitting streak is still a record in the National League, but it was tied by Pete Rose in 1978. He batted .424 in 1897, a mark that ranks third highest in all time for the majors. His lifetime batting average of .341 is among the top 15 in baseball history. He choked up on his bat so high that the Tigers' Sam Crawford claimed that "it seemed like he used only half of it."

Brickyard Kennedy pitched 12 seasons in the majors, 10 of them with Brooklyn. The right-hander won 20 games four times, compiling a career record of 187 wins. A tremendous workhorse, Kennedy threw over 300 innings five times. In 1900, he gave Brooklyn 292 innings, plus a couple of shutouts.

Brooklyn's Frank Kitson worked in an obscure era of baseball history. The national economy was in a hole in the early 20th century. Baseball memorabilia was seldom issued and, when it was, the result was unmemorable. As a result, we have to be grateful for anything depicting Kitson. This portrait was taken just before he moved to Brooklyn for the 1900 season, where he won 19 games in both 1901 and 1902.

The statistics for Deacon McGuire take up almost half a page in the baseball encyclopedia. He put on a uniform for 26 total seasons, calling games from behind the plate for nine different teams. He was in Brooklyn for three years, until 1901. He is pictured here a few years later in a New York Highlanders uniform.

"Wild Bill" Donovan was only 23 when he came to Brooklyn to pitch in 1899. He was with the team for few games in his first two seasons. In 1901, however, he led the National League with a 25-16 record. He started more games that year than any other pitcher (45) and established himself as a solid professional. He played a total of 18 years in the bigs.

While leagues were coming and going, and franchises were moving from city to city, the game of baseball, for blacks, was proceeding in a parallel universe. Racial segregation ensured that African American ballplayers would not share the field with their white counterparts. However, blacks did find a way to play, even as early as the turn of the century. The Brooklyn Royal Giants, shown in 1906, were an independent team playing up and down the East Coast. This photograph shows them in their first year, four seasons before they were to win the Eastern championship. The most famous player this year was Grant "Home Run" Johnson (third from left, back row). It is always fun to speculate how these talented athletes would have fared against their city's counterparts. It took more than 50 years before this injustice was addressed, but it was in Brooklyn where the first steps were taken.

The 1906 season saw a managerial turnover in Brooklyn, with Ned Hanlon leaving and Patsy Donovan coming over from Washington, where he managed. The team moved from last place to fifth in 1906, but little improvement occurred over the next few years. After 1908, Donovan was gone.

Jimmy Sheckard's rookie year was 1897, and he joined Brooklyn for 13 games. He became a starter the following year and stayed with the franchise until 1905. Sheckard was an outfielder more remembered for his time with the Chicago Cubs. His most remarkable statistic while in New York City was a league-leading slugging percentage of .534 in 1901.

A right-handed hurler from Dayton, Ohio, Harry McIntire started his big-league life in Brooklyn in 1905. He worked in the borough for five seasons, victorious in 46 games for the Superbas. His best record was in 1906, when he won 13 games. However, the teams he pitched for struggled, and McIntire never had a winning season in Brooklyn.

During Tim Jordan's brief career as a first baseman, his best years were playing for the Brooklyn Superbas. From 1906 to 1909, Jordan was a starter, impressing fans with his slugging exploits. This time period was called the "dead-ball era." In 1906 and 1908, he led the dead-ball National League in home runs, hitting 12 in each campaign.

Brooklyn Base Ball Club. National League.
Finished 5th. Won 66. Lost 86. Pct. .434.

1 Bergen.	5 Casey.	9 McCarthy.	13 Stricklett.
2 Hummel.	6 Eason.	10 Lewis.	14 Lumley.
3 Maloney.	7 McIntyre.	11 Jordan.	15 Owen.
4 Donovan (Mgr.)	8 Ritter.	12 Pastorius.	16 Batch.
	17 Alperman.		

The 1907 Brooklyn club was not particularly talented, finishing fifth in the league with a 65-83 record. Nevertheless, this team collage gives us a nice visual record of the players that year. Patsy Donovan was manager, the ex-Baltimore players had moved on, and the team lacked any star power. Tim Jordan (whose .274 average led the team's regulars) and Harry McIntire joined their teammates in this arrangement from the 1908 Spalding guide. Jim Pastorius won 16 games in 1907. George Napoleon Rucker (not included here) won 15, and Elmer Stricklett walked off with 12 victories. This was a club with little hope for success. With few changes occurring in personnel over the next seasons, Brooklyn fans would have to wait for the next decade to see a turnaround in the team's success. In 1908, they finished seventh. They finished sixth in 1909 and 1910.

George Napoleon Rucker, known as Nap, was described by many sportswriters of the day as the finest left-handed pitcher in the National League. Rucker, purchased from the South Atlantic League's Augusta club for a whopping $500, came to Brooklyn in 1907. He had won 27 games for Augusta, leading them to a pennant in 1906. He went on to spend his entire major-league career with the franchise. From 1907 to 1913, he won 15, 17, 13, 17, 22, 18, and 14 games, consecutively. The stocky, redheaded southpaw was a strikeout artist who led the league in shutouts in 1910 and 1912. Rucker hung on just long enough to see the team finally win a pennant, but his best days were past. He participated in only nine games in 1916. He won 134 games for four different managers and appeared in nearly 2,400 innings.

Another pitcher for the Dodgers *c.* 1910 was George Bell. He arrived in the big leagues at the age of 32. In his five years with Brooklyn, he was never given much support. For example, his dismal 10-27 record in 1910 was accompanied by a fine earned run average of 2.64.

In 1897, Ned Hanlon's Orioles were barnstorming in California when Jim Hughes of Sacramento shut out the tourists on three hits. Hanlon immediately signed Hughes and brought him back east. He won 60 games for the Superbas over three years. His best season was 1899, when he posted a 28-6 record with a winning percentage of .824, tops in the league.

Charlie Ebbets's Horatio Alger story saw him start as the Brooklyn club's bookkeeper. Over 15 years, he accumulated a majority number of shares and, in 1898, took over as president of the organization. He thought he could manage, but his 1898 team finished a miserable 10th place. Hanlon moved in the following year but, by 1905, wanted to move the franchise back to Baltimore. At that point, Ebbets bought Hanlon out. Ebbets became a popular personality in Brooklyn, where he developed the rain check ticket and a creative plan for drafting players that promoted parity in the league. By selling off half his ownership of the team to a pair of contractors (the McKeever brothers), Ebbets was able to finance the construction of a new ballpark in 1912. The stadium bore his name and became Brooklyn's home away from home.

Four
1910–1919

The good feelings the winning teams generated at the turn of the century did not last out the decade. Losing became as predictable by 1910 as winning had been 10 years earlier. The fans and the franchise needed revitalization. They needed to work out the kinks and bring home a winner. Here, the Dodgers exercise military style in spring training. It was not until 1916 that the Dodgers again claimed the title of champions. They entered the decade with a good core of players but lacked the positional strength needed to move higher in the National League. While the team was staying at Washington Park, refurbished and updated for the 1912 season, the ownership was willing to make changes necessary to bring a winner to Brooklyn. It took a while, but success was on the way.

SUPERBAS

Z.D. Wheat

OF THE
BROOKLYN NATIONALS

In the second decade of the 20th century, the American economy was improving. More products were being issued, and there was more competition. There was also more money for premiums and promotions that baseball fans always liked. Thus, cigarette companies decided to bring back the tobacco baseball card in 1908. They were printed in vast quantities and were very popular. In 1911, this design was issued for Hassan cigarettes. Zach Wheat is depicted in the card to the left. Bill Dahlen, Brooklyn's manager from 1910 to 1913, is shown below. Dahlen failed to pull the team out of its doldrums. He brought in finishes of sixth in 1910, seventh in 1911, seventh in 1912, and sixth in 1913.

SUPERBAS

H. F. Dahlen

OF THE
BROOKLYN NATIONALS

Zach Wheat arrived from Louisiana in 1909 and stayed in Brooklyn for 19 seasons, playing only one year elsewhere. He holds a stack of team records, including hits, doubles, triples, and games played. He accumulated 2,884 hits by the time he retired in 1927, with a lifetime batting mark of .317. In 13 seasons, this line-drive artist hit .300 or more, won the batting title in 1918 with .335, hit 132 home runs in this dead-ball era, and showed his speed by racking up 205 stolen bases. His production jumped markedly after 1921, when baseballs were more tightly wound, resulting in a livelier game. He began to hit home runs, where doubles were before. Never tallying more than nine home runs before, he blasted 16 in 1922 and 14 in each of three seasons, 1921, 1924, and 1925. Wheat was a mainstay in left field until he departed in 1926. His brother Mack sporadically caught for the club from 1915 to 1919.

On these two pages are two of the giants who took the mound for Brooklyn in the second decade of the 20th century. Ed Reulbach, shown here in 1914, stood six feet one inch and dominated National League batters for the Chicago Cubs for nine previous seasons. He won 116 games in Chicago and became the cornerstone of their pitching staff. His winning percentage topped all others in 1906 and 1907. Brooklyn thought he had something left when they picked him up in the middle of the 1913 season. He won 7 games for Bill Dahlen that year and 11 more the next. Although he put 21 wins in his pocket playing in the 1915 Federal League, his best days were over. Reulbach earned a total of 182 wins and was briefly a piece in the Superba puzzle.

46

Richard William "Rube" Marquard always looked big and gangly in pictures but must have been a terror on the mound. He was John McGraw's prize, next to Christy Mathewson, when they threw together for the New York Giants in Manhattan. He won 20 games three times for the Giants and participated in the 1911, 1912, and 1913 World Series. Thriving on postseason play, Marquard wanted to be back with his former pitching coach, Wilbert Robinson, who became Brooklyn manager in 1914. He got McGraw to agree and negotiated his departure from New York for $7,500. Rube found himself back in the Fall Classic in 1916, losing two games for Brooklyn, as the Red Sox won four games to one. He won 19 games in 1917, followed by two years plagued by injuries. He came back in 1920 to win 10 games for the team, helping them into the World Series, where he saw action in two games against the Cleveland Indians.

This magnificent action photograph was taken at Washington Park, probably *c*. 1912. The Cubs were in town and (if the photograph was taken in 1912) Tinker, Evers, and Chance, the famous double-play combination, would be on the field. The Brooklyn batter has just popped the pitch up. His teammates, leading off first and second bases, are deciding whether to move on or go back to safety. The pitcher, who looks like Three-Finger Brown, and the second

baseman are both moving for the ball. The detail is so great that we can clearly see the billboards advertising Ever-Ready razor blades, Pepsin Gum, and several brands of cigarettes and whiskey. We can also see the fans on the fire escapes and at the windows of the apartment building just beyond the right-field fence.

The Brooklyn Royal Giants continued playing. They entered a strong nine into the championship series each season. They claimed the national title in 1910, 1914, and 1916. There was also a Negro League World Series in 1916, in which the Royal Giants represented the East, and the Chicago American Giants represented the West. This 1914 photograph includes Louis Santop (back row, second from left), the club's starting catcher. Doc Sykes, Frank Wickware, Dizzy Dismukes, and Frank Harvey were the pitchers. Phil Bradley covered first that year, along with Bill Handy at second, Jesse Bragg at third, Dell Clark at shortstop, with Pop Andrews, Johnny Pugh, and Ernest Gatewood in the outfield. Brooklyn had another team in 1914—the Brooklyn All Stars, a franchise that lasted but one year. Not surprisingly, no photographs of that team have survived.

Wilbert "Uncle Robby" Robinson, an optimistic fixture in the Brooklyn dugout until 1931, was hired in 1914. He came over from the New York Giants, where he served under Mugsy McGraw. He immediately showed an ability to inspire and control his players simultaneously. Brooklyn finished fifth in Robinson's first year in power, third in 1915, followed by the pennant in 1916. Moving the team into contention in only three years excited the fans in Brooklyn, and they showed their gratitude by filling the ballpark once again. To show their affection for Robinson's role in the ascendancy of the club, the fans and newspapers began calling them "the Robins." Robinson is shown here in his handsome checkered uniform, shaking hands with Yankee manager Wild Bill Donovan, late of Brooklyn. The two team leaders were discussing ground rules before a preseason exhibition game.

The year 1916 was critical for Wilbert Robinson because he knew he had the personnel to take the National League flag. The pennant had been won by a different team in each of the past four years, with the Giants becoming champions in 1913, the Miracle Braves following in 1914, and the surprising Phillies in 1915. The general equality of talent in the league helped the Robins' chances. With his 1916 roster generating more hits than any other team (1,366) and carrying the highest batting average (.261), they still finished a mere two and a half games ahead of the Phillies. Robinson developed a close relationship with his players, both while in New York and in Brooklyn, helping continue the winning ways that owner Charlie Ebbets had in mind when he signed the new manager. Here, the team poses in Ebbets Field before an afternoon contest early in the 1916 season.

Harry "Jake" Daubert was an extraordinary first baseman, spending more that half of his 15-year career with Brooklyn. A National Leaguer from start to finish, he had a .303 lifetime average and was batting champion for the Superbas in 1913 at .350 and in 1914 at .329. With a glove, Daubert was just as good. His nimble play allowed him to average 10.5 assists and put-outs per game, with a fabulous fielding percentage hovering between .989 and .994 from 1910 to 1918. If he had been able to play a few more solid seasons, he would have had Hall of Fame numbers. Daubert knew his own value and sued Ebbets for money denied him by the owner after the 1918 season was shortened by about 20 games during World War I. Losing the settlement, an angry Ebbets traded Daubert to Cincinnati for Tommy Griffith, who played the outfield well but was no replacement for Daubert.

This classic photograph, taken during the 1916 World Series, shows the only scoring action in the second game. Henry Harrison "Hy" Myers is seen leaving the batter's box after stroking the ball to the wall in the first inning. The speedy Myers circled the bases for an inside-the-park home run, the Robins' only run scored in the game against Boston lefty Babe Ruth. After the Red Sox tied the game at 1-1, Ruth and Sherry Smith battled for 10 scoreless innings, with the final 2-1 American League victory coming in the 14th inning. Boston dominated this World Series, winning four games to one and holding the opposition to only 13 total runs. Jack Coombs won the only game for Wilbert Robinson, whose squad had been held to a team batting average of .200 for the series. However, the fans were happy, since postseason play had returned to Brooklyn.

All New Yorkers know of Charles Dillon "Casey" Stengel, but not many know he had a playing and managerial career. Stengel was an outfielder who came up with Brooklyn in 1912. His nickname came from his home town of Kansas City. He was to stay for seven years, starting for the club each of them. Not yet known as "the Old Professor," he was learning the game from top to bottom, knowledge that he carried into his post-playing career, when he led the New York Yankees to championships year in and year out in the 1950s and 1960s. He could be a hot-head when appropriate but could also be coolly analytical. Stengel was one of the bright spots in the 1916 World Series, leading the team with a .364 batting average. In early January 1918, Stengel and infielder George Cutshaw were traded to the Pittsburgh Pirates for pitcher Burleigh Grimes, pitcher Al Mamaux, and utility infielder Chuck Ward. (Courtesy Marshall Fogel.)

Zach Wheat's beautiful swing is shown to great effect in this full-length photograph. Wheat stood 5 feet 10 inches and weighed 170 pounds. Like his father before him, he operated a farm in Missouri, where he stayed every off-season until he had to sell the property during the Great Depression. He had begun his career by tending outfields in Mobile, Alabama, and in Shreveport, Louisiana. A Dodger scout found and signed him while performing near New Orleans. He played in the World Series twice with the Robins, in 1916 and 1920. In these years, he did some of his finest hitting. He consistently rapped out about 175 hits, knocked in about 75 runs, scored about the same, and batted .300. Manager Robinson could always count on Wheat to anchor the outfield and hit in the clutch.

Right-handed pitcher Leon Cadore came to Robinson's team in 1915 but did not work a full season with them until 1917, when he went 13-13. He improved that win total in 1919 and 1920 with 14 and 15, respectively. All 68 of his career wins were earned in Brooklyn. He started one game in the 1920 World Series and relieved in another.

Smack in the middle of his pitching career, Al Mamaux found himself in Brooklyn, having come over from Pittsburgh in the fall of 1917. He had won 21 games for the Pirates twice. Robinson was hoping he could duplicate that feat in Brooklyn, but it was not to be. Mamaux did bring home 12 victories in 1920 and got to work in the World Series against Cleveland. However, he only won four more games in Brooklyn in the next three years.

A chubby, elflike Wilbert Robinson speaks with his temperamental star southpaw, Rube Marquard. He knew how to talk to Marquard and how to make his delivery as smooth as "the glide," a dance step Rube performed with his movie star wife. In this view, Marquard looks like he is concentrating on getting in that groove by blowing hard with his eyes shut. This was the real pregame warm-up. Robinson coaxed quite a career out of Marquard, as his pitching coach and then as his manager. As the 1920 season ended, however, Robinson was not sure how much was left in that long left arm. In 1921, as manager Robinson was leading the Robins into a new decade, Big Rube left for Cincinnati.

Five

1920–1929

The year 1920 marked the second time in five years that Wilbert Robinson took Brooklyn to the World Series. A number of players had great years, and the stars of the team performed at predictable levels. They finished a healthy seven games ahead of the number two Giants and led the league in earned run average. Although they did not achieve the honors in home runs, hits, runs batted in, or other offensive stats, they played tightly as a team, making their runs count and strategically taking every advantage. They had three .300 hitters—outfielders Zach Wheat and Hi Myers plus the new first baseman, veteran Ed Konechy. The team batting average was .277. Burleigh Grimes and Al Mamaux (pitchers who were picked up a few years earlier) chipped in 23 and 12 wins, respectively. All in all, it was a great summer for the Robins, and the fans had now come to think of their uniformed heroes as winners, capable of competing each and every year.

Dutch Ruether was probably of German descent but, after World War I, it was preferable to hail from Holland. His beginning years in the majors were with Cincinnati, where he won 19 games in 1919, stayed in the rotation during the World Series, with a complete game victory in one of his two starts. The year 1921 found Ruether in a new uniform and in the always changing borough of Brooklyn. A left-hander by nature, he won a total of 54 games with the Robins. His best season was 1922, when he won 22 with a 3.53 earned run average. A fine batsman as well, Ruether had a lifetime batting average .258. He is fifth on the list for pinch hits by a pitcher. By 1923, Brooklyn had a formidable pitching staff, with Ruether joined by Burleigh Grimes and Dazzy Vance. There was stability with the team, most of all because Wilbert Robinson would outlast the 1920s as manager.

Ed "Koney" Konechy came over to Brooklyn in 1919 and continued to play a solid first base in 1920 and 1921. He would always bat about .300, play about 130 games, and anchor an infield of journeymen. He had made his mark in St. Louis, where he broke into big-time baseball at 22 years of age. He was an iron man and defensive stalwart throughout his 15-year career.

Spitball-throwing Burleigh Grimes was not committing a crime, at least when his career was young. Grimes and a few other notorious spitballers could throw truly untouchable curve balls, but eventually the practice was stopped. His technique was honed in Pittsburgh for two years before launching a Hall of Fame career in Brookyn. He won more games for the Dodgers than for any other team.

Through many seasons working under Wilbert Robinson, "Old Stubblebeard" Grimes was a league leader in many categories. He won over 20 games for Brooklyn four times and twice led the league in innings pitched. As a Dodger, he also led the league in complete games three times, in strikeouts once, in winning percentage once, and in victories once. The workhorse started three games in the 1920 World Series but only claimed a 1-2 record.

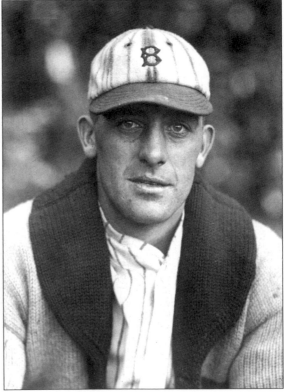

Charlie Hargreaves even looked like one of the haggard, overworked, hard-bitten, and unappreciated catchers that have always been with us. For six seasons in Brooklyn, he toiled in the "tools of ignorance," as catcher's gear is called, never playing more than 85 games in a season. Nevertheless, the Robins' fans loved him to the point of bombarding George Harper of the Phillies after a collision with Hargreaves the inning before.

Clarence Arthur Vance was known as Dazzy, and the Brooklyn team was known as the Daffiness Boys. Vance had a checkered past before coming to the Robins in 1922. He stood 6 feet 2 inches tall, weighed 200 pounds, and had been an exclusively fastball pitcher in the minor leagues. He bounced from franchise to franchise until a successful operation for arm soreness brought him around and a Brooklyn scout advised his signing for the 1922 season.

Vance had developed a good curve ball and a baffling windup, employing a high leg kick, the ball hidden in his huge palm, with his intentionally tattered red undershirt flapping distractingly. His new technique worked well, and this 31-year-old rookie was off and running. He led the National League in strikeouts seven straight seasons, starting in 1922. He notched over 20 wins for Wilbert Robinson three times. His best year was 1924, when he won 28 games.

Seasons came and went as the franchise moved into the 1920s. The pennant won in 1920 brought dreams of continued success, but it was never easy. The 1921 club ended up in fifth place, winning only two games more than they lost. In 1922, despite the arrival of Dazzy Vance, they dropped to sixth and dipped under the .500 mark in winning percentage. The following year was a statistical duplicate, as again they came in sixth. Robinson worked the team hard. Every spring training, he figured to get the most out of his roster, teaching technique to pitchers and hitters alike. Unfortunately for the Robins, Mugsy McGraw had put together a winning Giants team in Manhattan. The New Yorkers took the flag in 1921, 1922, 1923, and 1924, leaving little but crumbs for the competition.

A great big boy is what Floyd Caves "Babe" Herman looked like in 1926, when he broke in as a rookie. The six-foot-four-inch hitter weighed 190 pounds and belted a career high of 35 homers for the Robins in 1930. His hitting skills were undeniable from the start, as he batted over .300 for each of his minor-league teams, including .416 average playing in two junior circuits in 1922. A core member of the Daffiness Boys, Herman often performed poorly in the field, offsetting his batting skills. He entertained the fans by booting the most balls at his position for two consecutive seasons (1927 and 1928), playing first base and then outfield. Things just seemed to happen to Herman and his teammates, such as the time one of Herman's drives to the fence resulted in three Brooklyn runners standing on third base together. This brought on the vaudeville joke "The Dodgers have three men on base!" "Really? Which base?" In this photograph, Herman is standing next to an established hitting terror for the Cubs, Hack Wilson, who moved to Brooklyn six years later.

Hired primarily for his defensive abilities, Jigger Statz ended his career in Brooklyn, playing for them in 1927 and 1928. He played 130 games in 1927 and batted a respectable .274. He had a few strong seasons with the Cubs a bit earlier but made minor-league history by playing for Los Angeles in the Pacific Coast League for 18 years.

Del Bissonette's rookie season was almost his best, as he belted 25 home runs and drove in 106. He was another of the good-hit-no-field phenoms that ended up at first base for Brooklyn in the 1920s. This limerick was overheard near Borough Hall: "The Dodgers have Del Bissonette, Not a meal has he ever missed yet. This question arises, bringing surprises: Who paid for all Del Bissonette?"

Max Carey came to Brooklyn after a disagreement with Pittsburgh management, his Hall of Fame numbers already behind him. He had starred in centerfield for the Pirates for 15 years, being the best in the National League at that position. He played a full season in 1927 but began spending more time as a teacher. He became Brooklyn's manager in 1932.

Jess Petty was known as "the Silver Fox" for his prematurely gray hair. He was a key figure in Wilbert Robinson's pitching rotation from 1926 to 1928, racking up well over 200 innings pitched each year. He led the team with 17 victories in 1926. After the 1928 season, he was sent to Pittsburgh, and he ended his career a year later.

67

Hall of Fame shortstop Dave Bancroft stopped off in Brooklyn for two years. He solidified the infield wherever he went. He was, however, 37 years old and had lost his speed and quickness. Another in a parade of fading stars the club acquired in the late 1920s, Bancroft did move on to one more team but retired after 10 games.

Cuban right-hander Adolfo Luque had blazed a trail for himself in the majors with Cincinnati for 12 campaigns, coming to play for Wilbert Robinson in 1930. He won 14 his first year and 7 the next. Luque, nicknamed "the Pride of Havana," was known as an explosive character, but he apparently got on well with his new manager.

As the decade wound down, Wilbert Robinson's Robins seemed to be going nowhere. Beginning in 1925, they finished sixth for five straight years, as if the spot in the standings was made for them. Workouts like this one—held during 1928 spring training in Clearwater, Florida—did not seem to do much good. "Wait till next year" became more of a joke than a lament on Flatbush Avenue. Ebbets Field was not packing them in, as was the case during the winning years. Some of the reliable old stars, such as Zach Wheat, were gone and no young prospects had blossomed into real replacements. However, patience was part of life in Brooklyn, and the fans followed the roster changes every year, debated acquisitions and managerial decisions, and kept on rooting for their boys, in sixth place or not.

Every once in a while, a pair of pictures will take over the imagination and become visually intertwined. Such is the case with these two photographs of instantaneous action at home plate (this page and next). This picture was taken in Brooklyn, the other in Philadelphia, but Dodgers are involved in each. Baseball games are remembered and recorded as moments of action, bursts of activity that determine outcomes and make history. These photographs seem

to show the same play, shot from separate angles simultaneously. Although they are clearly different pictures, they reveal how like and unlike baseball games are, and how new and how repetitive the activity is. In the photograph to the left, Brooklyn's Fred Walker scoots home as the Cardinals' Don Padgett leaps for the throw. In the image above, we see Glenn Wright scoring while the Phillies' Spud Davis jumps behind him.

Taking aim on the 1930s are a couple of Brooklyn sluggers who showed up after the Wilbert Robinson era had ended. The team was called the Dodgers exclusively again, and hopes for improvement were entertained, if not warranted. Hack Wilson (right) was as strong as an ox and built like a diminutive brick wall. He signed with the Dodgers in 1932, having astonished the baseball world two years before by driving in an inconceivable 190 runs. Wilson only played for 12 seasons, his last productive ones being in Brooklyn. In that stretch of time, however, he put up numbers sufficient for a Hall of Fame induction. Len Koenecke (next to Wilson) showed promise in his first two seasons with the Dodgers. He hit .320 with 14 home runs in 1934. However, he had behavioral problems. After Dodger manager Casey Stengel released Koenecke in September 1935, he took a flight home. On the way, he got drunk, accosted the pilot and co-pilot, and was hit on the head and killed. He was only 31.

Six

1930–1939

This photograph, taken before a game at Ebbets Field in June 1930, shows a nice lineup for the Dodgers. Babe Herman looks unhappy at the far left—or perhaps it is an expression of the determination he used to pound the ball from April to October that year. He not only drove in runs but also scored 143 and banged out 241 hits. Johnny Frederick (second from the left) only tended the Ebbets Field garden in his major-league career, but they were six productive years, starting in 1929. Del Bissonette is posed in the middle. To his left is Jake Flowers, a utility infielder and a jinx against teams that traded him. On the far right is Al Lopez, a smart and hardworking catcher, who would call games for the club until 1935. Lopez became an accomplished manager for the Indians and the White Sox and was elected to the National Baseball Hall of Fame in 1977.

The Roaring Twenties were over, the economy was depressed, and it sometimes seemed that playing big-league ball was just another dirty job. In this September 4, 1931 photograph, the two rivals—the Giants and Dodgers—are playing at the Polo Grounds, uptown in Manhattan. The dust is still rising after a close play at the plate, and the umpire has become the center of attention. Johnny Frederick is flying by but has just been tagged out by the Giants' catcher, Shanty Hogan. Someone is already arguing the call behind the umpire. Hogan is starting to smile, and the umpire knows he got it right. It is just another day of hard labor at the ball yards.

Max Carey and his equally well-dressed son welcome Hack Wilson to the Dodgers before the start of the 1932 season. Carey had taken over managerial duties from Wilbert Robinson the previous winter, and Wilson was no doubt key in Carey's plans for the Dodgers into the future. Carey boosted the team to third place with a respectable eight games over .500.

The Dodgers employed a number of shortstops in the 1930s. Among them was Jimmy Jordan, entering in 1933 and exiting three years later. He had been batting champion in the Central League (1928) and then MVP in the Sally League (1930). Although he came with credentials, Lonny Frey and Glenn Wright took most of the playing time.

The Dodgers gave up Lefty O'Doul and Watty Clark for Sam Leslie in 1933, but he was the one Max Carey wanted to solidify his infield at first base. Leslie was more a hitter than a fielder. He had an average of .286 in 96 games in 1933, of .332 in 146 games in 1934, and of .308 in 142 games in 1935.

Journeyman third baseman Joe Stripp signed contracts with Brooklyn from 1932 to 1937, batting over .300 four of the six seasons. He was a starter throughout his career, playing the hot corner steadily. In the off-seasons, he operated the Jersey Joe Stripp's Baseball School, training ambitious young ballplayers in Orlando, Florida.

There are always more players than are needed at spring training—including plenty of catchers, a position that really wears a player down. These three backstops for Casey Stengel's Dodgers got past the cut and spent the whole of the 1934 season together. Al Lopez (left) claimed the starter's role, with 140 games behind the plate. Clyde Sukeforth (center) participated in 27 games, and Ray Berres played in 39. Sukeforth had only one 100-game season (1931) but did stay on as Dodger coach for many years. He even served shortly as interim manager in 1941, after Leo Durocher was dismissed. Lopez was a marvel, as the records do show. His 114 games without a passed ball in 1941 was a record. He led the National League's catchers in assists for three years and led all catchers in fielding three times. His lifetime batting average was .261, but he still would have kept his job with a total 20 points lower.

Dazzy Vance is pictured wearing the 1932 design of the Dodgers uniform, which had undergone quite a few changes since he had started pitching for the team 10 years before. This was Vance's last full year with the team, and he was to win 12 games. A huge favorite at Ebbets Fields, Vance won 189 games for his fans and had a great time doing it. In 1924, he had won an MVP award in the National League, beating out .424-hitting Rogers Hornsby. That year, Vance threw 30 complete games, won 28 of them, with only six games lost and an earned run average of 2.16. He did his best to get Brooklyn into a World Series, but the team lost out to the Giants by one game that year. After 1924, he never again came close to postseason play.

The Dodgers are back at spring training in 1932. Dodger outfielders are getting a good workout, rookie and veteran alike. A red-faced Hack Wilson is upside down, second from the left. Lefty O'Doul, who spent a couple of summers with the Dodgers, is burning fat on the far right.

This photograph offers one last look at Dazzy Vance, who is showing some age after a 16-year career. He treated the fans to a no-hitter in 1924, dozens of team records, and an all-around good time when he pitched. The Brooklyn faithful would miss him, always enjoying his round, smiling face and his antics on the mound.

Lonny Frey was the starting shortstop in Brooklyn from 1934 to 1936. He was a speedy, slick fielder and put together a solid 14-year career. He only apprenticed with the Dodgers, playing in three All-Star games and one World Series with the Reds, the team he was traded to in 1937.

Long, tall Len Koenecke stretches for a high one in a posed 1935 spring training photograph. He was coming off a fine season, in which he had a .411 on-base percentage and a slugging percentage over .500. In 1932, at age 28, he was considered old for a rookie. The 1935 season was to be his last.

Brooklyn Eagles - Jacksonville, Florida. April 2nd 1935

At the same time that Frenchie Bordagaray was arriving in Brooklyn and Johnny Frederick was leaving, the Brooklyn Eagles were playing their one and only season in the Negro National League. A total of 47 players appeared on the team's roster that summer, giving Abe Manley a chance to look at lots of baseball talent. After the season, he bought this club as well as the Newark Dodger franchise and then combined them into a single team he called the Newark Eagles. This group showed the best the team had to offer. They are, from left to right, as follows: (front row) Bobby Williams, unidentified, Tex Burnett, Dennis Gilcrest, ? Ward, and Leon Day; (back row) Ben Taylor, C.B. Griffin, Ted Page, Lamon Yokely, unidentified, George Giles, unidentified, Harry Williams, and Ted Radcliffe. Leon Day stayed an Eagle, playing for Newark until 1939. The best pitcher on the team, Day was a right-handed fastballer who was counted on for strikeouts.

Buddy Hassett was languishing in the minor leagues, waiting for Lou Gehrig to retire. Finally, in 1936, the Yankees traded him to Brooklyn, where he took over first base, hitting .310 in 156 games. The Yankees wanted him back but could not arrange it until his final season, in 1942. Hassett hit .300 twice for the Dodgers, before he was traded to the Boston Braves in 1939.

Before hanging up his cleats for good, Van Lingle Mungo had won 120 games in the majors. Most of those were for Brooklyn, where he arrived in 1931 and stayed for a decade. His most productive years were 1932 through 1936, when he won 13, 16, 18, 16, and 18, respectively.

Most pictures of George "Moose" Earnshaw were taken when he was a pitching star for the Philadelphia Athletics in the American League. Earnshaw stood six feet four inches tall and weighed just over 200 pounds. He had won 20 games three straight years in Philadelphia and won 12 in two years in Brooklyn (adding together his wins in 1935 and 1936).

Feisty George Magerkurth was in the middle of many battles during his major-league umpiring career. He never backed down from a fight, as is surely the case in this April 1937 photograph. The Dodgers are both giving and getting an earful in this dispute at third base in a game against the perpetually disliked Giants.

Johnny Cooney logged 20 major-league seasons, mostly in the outfield. He labored for the Boston Braves until his last two years, when he came to Brooklyn. He was a .286 lifetime hitter, but his hit total of 965 hits demonstrates that he was a starter for only part of his career.

It was near the end of the 1930s when Dolph Camili was pursued and brought to Brooklyn by general manager Larry MacPhail. Camili immediately became a local favorite, especially in Brooklyn's Italian community. He won the MVP award as a Dodger for his remarkable 1941 season. That year, he led the National League in home runs and runs batted in, while smoothly handling his duties at first base.

Pitcher Burleigh Grimes turned in his glove for a lineup card when he took over as Dodger manager in 1937. Stengel had not been able to do much with the team, and Grimes's confrontational manner did little to boost morale or improve the winning percentage. Grimes lasted only two years at the helm, leaving at the end of 1938 and giving way to an equally troublesome Leo Durocher.

The Boston Braves sent Freddie Frankhouse, age 32, to the Dodgers after the close of the 1935 season. He had been an All-Star in Beantown, winning 17 games in 1934. His arm still had some life in Brooklyn, winning 13 in 1936 (along with a nifty 3.65 earned run average) and 10 in 1937.

Henry "Heinie" Manush (far left) was Brooklyn's biggest acquisition for the 1937 season. Having starred for the Tigers and Senators in the American League, Manush's left-handed batting skills were to bolster a lineup that landed the Dodgers in seventh place in 1936. A perennial .300 hitter, Manush won only one batting title, beating out Babe Ruth in 1926 with a .378 average. He poses with three of his teammates in this pregame photograph. They are, from left to right, John Cooney, Tom Winsett, and Fred Frankhouse. Cooney was in his "second" career as an outfielder, sharing the wide-open spaces with Tom Winsett, who before and after this year served as a substitute only. He had hit 50 home runs for Columbus in the American Association, and the Dodgers thought they might have a star aborning. However, his highest major-league total was the five homers he hit in 1937.

A smiling Leo Durocher was an unusual sight. If things were not going perfectly, he would take your head off. Even as a middle infielder, Durocher was a confrontational competitor who could not stand losing. He played for the Yankees, Reds, and Cardinals before he reached Brooklyn. Although he put in six seasons with the club as a player, he is remembered almost exclusively for his managing.

Whitlow Wyatt arrived in Brooklyn in 1939, the first of six seasons there. In 1940, he tied for the league lead in shutouts, with five. A year later, he won 22 games, to match teammate Kirby Higbe. He was always known as an aggressive knockdown artist. After watching him in action, Joe DiMaggio called him the "meanest man" he had ever seen.

The Dodgers' brain trust seems to be conspiring at their spring training site at Bear Mountain, New York. Restrictions on train travel during World War II kept the Dodgers from training in Florida, and the Westchester County State Park made a reasonable replacement. Leo Durocher (in uniform) had become the Dodger skipper in 1939, and Branch Rickey (with him on the bench) became club president a few years later. They often worked well together, but working with Durocher was always a challenge. Before Rickey arrived, Durocher won a pennant for the Dodgers in 1941. However, the team moved one notch down in 1942 and again in 1943. They bounced around in the standings through the rest of Durocher's term, ending with a second-place finish in 1946. Durocher went to spring training with the team in 1947 and distinguished himself by putting down a revolt against the hiring of Jackie Robinson. A league suspension for the 1947 season came in early April, after Durocher was accused of associating with gamblers.

Seven
1940–1949

The 1941 pennant was gratifying for Larry MacPhail, who was the Dodgers' general manager and president until the arrival of Branch Rickey in 1943. The fiery MacPhail knew the team needed more talent to make up the 12 games that they were trailing in 1940, behind National League champion Cincinnati Reds. He picked up catcher Mickey Owen from the Cardinals, second baseman Billy Herman from the Cubs, and pitcher Kirby Higbe from the Phillies. Plus, he added veteran pitchers Johnny Allen, Mace Brown, and Newt Kimball, who together won nine games in 1941. The real prize was Higbe, whose 22-9 record was a highlight in the Dodger season. He led the league in wins and in games (48), all of them starts. The National League champions are, from left to right, as follows: (front row) trainer Wilson, Cookie Lavagetto, Pee Wee Reese, Pete Reiser, coach Red Corriden, manager Leo Durocher, coach Chuck Dressen, Kirby Higbe, Mickey Owen, Lew Riggs, and mascot Bodner; (middle row) Ducky Medwick, Curt Davis, Tom Drake, Larry French, Whitt Wyatt, Ed Albosta, Luke Hamlin, Newt Kimball, Billy Herman, and Johnny Allen; (back row) Hugh Casey, Dolph Camili, George Pfister, James Wasdell, Herman Franks, coach Spencer, Pete Coscorat, Freddie Fitzsimmons, Augie Galan, and Dixie Walker.

The second-place Dodgers of 1940 included Cookie Lavagetto (left) at third; baby-faced Pee Wee Reese (middle), who shared shortstop duties with manager Durocher; and first baseman Dolph Camili (right), who chalked up 142 games played that year. The last piece of the infield puzzle for the 1941 season was the acquisition of Billy Herman, to solidify second base.

Shortly before going after Herman, MacPhail acquired Curt Davis, a tall, lanky right-hander who had been working for the Cardinals. He had won 22 in 1939 but was known more for his durability. He won 13 games for the Dodgers in 1941. He started game one of the World Series against the Yankees, losing a close one 3-2.

This frozen moment records a double play in progress during game three of the 1941 World Series. This subway series with the Yankees was an exciting one for Brooklyn, even if the results were not pleasing. It had been 21 years since the Dodgers saw postseason play, and the faithful at Ebbets got to see the last three of the five games at home. Whitt Wyatt earned the only victory, starting game two for Brooklyn. Although Curt Davis started game one, Wyatt's success put him on the mound against the Yankees' Tiny Bonham for game five. The most memorable incident of the series was catcher Mickey Owen's muffed third strike in game four. Hugh Casey relieved in the fifth and held the Yankees down until there were two out in the ninth inning. Casey struck out Tommy Henrich for what should have been a Dodger victory, but Owen did not handle the pitch. The ball went to the screen, sending Henrich to first. After Casey gave up a single, two doubles, and two walks, the series was over.

Hall of Famer Joe "Ducky" Medwick came to prominence with the St. Louis Cardinals' Gashouse Gang of the 1930s. His hitting feats included a league-leading number of runs batted in between 1936 and 1938. After a sub-par 1939 season, the Dodgers bought him. He had a solid season in 1941, a big part of the pennant push that year.

This superb action photograph shows Mickey Owen reaching for a foul pop on opening day at Ebbets Field. Fans duck, dodge, and wince as Owen lunges, but the ball gets away. It seems the 1941 season began for Owen much the way it ended in the World Series against the Yankees.

Many fans and baseball insiders alike thought Pete Reiser was the greatest baseball talent they had ever seen. Coming up for his first full season in 1941, he won the National League batting crown at the youngest age ever, 22. The biggest surprise of the year (and a new face that clearly helped put the Dodgers over the top), Reiser also led the league in runs, doubles, triples, and slugging percentage. He played the game with utter abandon, with no concern to his health or safety, which eventually brought his downfall. He had to be carried off the field more than 10 times after injuries, mostly from full-speed encounters with the outfield wall. In this busy Ebbets Field photograph, Reiser congratulates Dolph Camili at the dugout after a September 1941 home run. Reiser's injury-shortened career ended in 1952, but he remained a favorite through the years with Dodger fans.

Even though the Yankees took the 1941 World Series 4-1, every game was close, and the result could easily have been reversed. The team had received the nickname "the Bums," an affectionate Brooklyn term that stuck with them until the end. Scrapping all the way, Leo Durocher always wanted desperately to win, sparing no opinions with his players or the umpires. A chance to enlighten three arbiters at once was welcome, as Durocher demonstrates here. He was technically a player-manager, but to get the Dodgers to the 100-win level where they finished, his on-field duties were organizational and argumentative. Brooklyn switched status with the Reds, champions the year before in the National League. In 1941, Cincinnati was 12 games behind the Dodgers, but they ended third, with the St. Louis Cardinals mounting the bigger threat, ending in second place at two and a half games back. Durocher's boys dominated the league in most offensive categories, scoring 800 runs, 103 better than the previous season. MacPhail's additions and Durocher's tenacity had paid off.

Pete Reiser was excitable, dedicated, and a little eccentric, but his enthusiasm was contagious, as shown in this wind-sprint exercise during the 1947 spring training. Reiser clearly loved playing ball and everything associated with it. He could be counted on to enliven the playing field and to energize the fans.

Reiser was an early supporter of Jackie Robinson, having met him during World War II military service at Fort Riley, Kansas. Before entering the military, Reiser led the league in stolen bases in 1942. That same year, Reiser is shown stealing home, showing off his hell-for-leather slide in a game against the Chicago Cubs. Clyde McCullough was the Cubs' catcher.

Fred "Dixie" Walker was known as "the People's Cherce" in Brooklyn, where he roamed the outfield from 1939 to 1947. A steady and productive hitter, he played the game hard, as demonstrated by this slide into third base against Boston in a 1940 contest. However, his confrontational opposition to Jackie Robinson in 1947 has somewhat tarnished his memory.

Announcer Red Barber—who had been hired away from Cincinnati shortly after Larry MacPhail took over as general manager in 1938—was beloved from day one. Broadcasting from "the catbird seat," Barber had a way with words and a charming voice, helping him to create more Dodger fans. He became synonymous with the Dodgers in the 1940s and 1950s.

This scene at Ebbets Field shortly before a game was reenacted 77 times a season. Before standing in line, you could grab a drink and a hotdog at a nearby stand and meet your friends at the gate. When Larry MacPhail arrived in Brooklyn, he found the Ebbets interior in serious disrepair. The money he raised immediately on arrival not only acquired important new talent for the team but restored and painted the grandstands. He was also to bring in lights in 1938, as the era of night games had begun. To attract crowds to the later starting games, he introduced various stunts and circuslike entertainments as pregame fare. The crowds responded well to the carnival atmosphere and filled the park regularly for MacPhail, even when the team was losing. MacPhail introduced Ladies Day, which was soon adopted by teams in both leagues.

Leo Durocher and cigar-smoking Branch Rickey do not seem too concerned about Durocher's suspension for all of the 1947 season. Durocher was known as a cardsharp, a horse-racing fan, and a reputed pal of gangster Bugsy Siegel. This harsh punishment came just before the April opener at Ebbets Field.

Despite Durocher's off-field problems, he got along with his players pretty well. He was a hard taskmaster but would put himself on the line for them at every opportunity. Standing at the batting cage during a break at 1946 spring training, Durocher (far left) entertains seven of his starters with some amusing tales of their trade.

This is one of a thousand pictures taken of Leo Durocher in a dispute with an umpire. There were probably more shots like this one than portraits of the Dodger skipper. Dixie Walker (upper left), Dolph Camili (upper right), and catcher Herman Franks join in the argument, but Durocher is doing most of the talking. Durocher was a player-manager in his first few years with the Dodgers but left the roster after 1941. Scenes like this one were reenacted almost daily, and his pugnacious nature proved troublesome for opponents and Dodger brass alike. After his one-year suspension in 1947, he returned to run the club in 1948. He installed rookie Roy Campanella, fresh from the Negro League, as catcher and moved Gil Hodges from behind the plate to first base. Nevertheless, the club floundered, and Durocher was fired by midseason. Burt Shotten, his replacement in 1947, came back as manager. Durocher never again wore a Dodger uniform.

In perhaps the most famous player signing in baseball history, Branch Rickey and Jackie Robinson exchange thoughts on the prospects for the revolutionary 1947 season. Carefully considered the player best suited to break baseball's color line, Robinson had the combination of superb playing ability and the temperament to tolerate the abuse and hostility that Rickey knew would be coming.

Burt Shotten's calm and confident demeanor made him an instant favorite with Dodger players after he took over for Leo Durocher, who was banned for the 1947 season. He was also able to unify the Dodgers behind Jackie Robinson while handling the sociological upheaval that his hiring produced. In this view, Shotten chats in the clubhouse with Robinson and outfielder Carl Furillo, who was in his second season with Brooklyn.

Hugh Casey was an effective relief pitcher, starting only 56 of the 343 career games he appeared in. He led the National League in relief victories on three occasions, and saves twice. He enjoyed Dodger spring training sessions south of the border. He is shown getting some midday rest in 1948 in Mexico. One year earlier, during a break in the March training activities in Havana, Cuba, Casey did some sparring with friend Ernest Hemingway.

Although Kirby Higbe was a flame-throwing right-hander, he appears to be demonstrating a knuckle ball grip in this portrait. Higbe had grown up with racial segregation in the South. Not at all happy about the arrival of Jackie Robinson, he grudgingly accepted the situation. He only shared the field with Robinson for a month, as he was traded to the Pirates in May 1947.

Jackie Robinson was a star athlete at UCLA, earning All-American honors in football. He also played baseball and basketball, but the national pastime offered him opportunities other games could not. He played some semiprofessional ball and then advanced to play shortstop in 1945 for the Kansas City Monarchs. He was instantly recognized as a fine infielder, a good batsman, and a speedy and smart base runner. In 1945, Branch Rickey signed Robinson to a Dodger contract, with the intention of assigning him to play a full season in Montreal, Brooklyn's triple-A franchise. First, however, Robinson was placed on an African American All-Star barnstorming team, off to tour Venezuela. The winter in South America done, Robinson headed for the Royals of Montreal. He batted .349 for the Canadian team, justifying the faith put in him by Rickey. As much as his on-field skills were under scrutiny, his demeanor and character were of greater importance.

After a successful full season north of the border, Robinson was brought to spring training with the major-league club. The first evidence of what was to come would surface that February and March, and Branch Rickey was ready for it. Consequently, Havana, Cuba, was chosen as the training site, since integrated baseball had been played there since the early 20th century. Leo Durocher had been thoroughly instructed as to what to expect. Although the situations presented were intense and new, Durocher did a good job. He pulled disgruntled players back into line, recognized those who would never accept Robinson, and discussed trading them with boss Rickey. Meanwhile, Robinson made the most of the city and the physical regimen. With fans who were black and white gathering around him, Robinson happily signed autographs and mingled in a society more racially integrated than his own.

103

Roy Campanella's route to the major league was eased by the appearance of Jackie Robinson in 1947. Campy started his career with the Baltimore Elite Giants at age 15. He played also in Puerto Rico and Cuba before his signing with the Dodgers brought him to minor-league venues in Nashua, New Hampshire, in 1946; Montreal, Canada, in 1947; and St. Paul, Minnesota, in 1948. By the end of the 1948 season, he was with the Bums for good.

One of the most famous incidents of early 1947 may have changed the direction of the season and perhaps the game of baseball itself. While on the road with the Dodgers, Robinson was being taunted by racist fans. Pee Wee Reese (pictured selecting a bat before heading to the plate) took a break between pitches, walked over to Robinson, and put his arm around his shoulder. It was a small gesture with a mighty impact.

Pee Wee Reese was obviously a player with a big heart and a tolerant spirit. If any player on the Dodgers helped make Rickey's experiment work, it was Reese. Harold Henry (his legal name) was a recognized leader, becoming Dodger captain shortly after arriving in 1940. His first full season was 1941, when his glove and bat work aided considerably in the team's victorious pennant drive. He was soon known as the National League's premiere shortstop, elected to the All-Star team annually from 1947 to 1954. His positive and generous nature was fully appreciated by his teammates and Dodger fans, as demonstrated by the birthday party thrown for him at Ebbets Field in 1955. He received more than $20,000 in gifts as 35,000 fans held candles and sang "Happy Birthday." The young fans who are gathered around Reese in this picture experience his generosity as he takes a break at Vero Beach spring training camp to sign some autographs.

The Dodgers' pennant in 1947 helped justify the signing of Robinson and began a new era in the major league and in the country. In the World Series, the Dodgers got closer to winning, taking three of the seven games this time. Dixie Walker, who would be gone after the World Series ended, crosses the plate in the fourth inning of game two with the first home run of the series.

In game six, the big event of the 1947 World Series occurred. The Bums were already down 3-2 in games and were on the brink of defeat. With the Yankees threatening to overtake the shaky Dodger lead in the late innings, Al Gionfriddo was sent into left field as a defensive substitute. DiMaggio promptly belted one to left, bidding for a home run. Gionfriddo and the ball arrived simultaneously at the outfield fence. The fabulous catch and resulting Dodger victory took the World Series to game seven, when the Yankees' Bill Bevens beat the Dodgers 5-2.

Change never comes without pain, and Jackie Robinson felt much of it. The brave and talented Dodger second baseman had to face verbal barbs from the stands and opposing dugouts, as well as beanballs in the batter's box. In this photograph, teammates and the trainer gather around as Robinson tries to recover from a fastball to the head.

The 1949 season brought another National League flag to Brooklyn, and they once again faced the Yankees in the October Classic. In Yankee Stadium the contest began, with Allie Reynolds on the mound, as seen in this photograph. Don Newcombe pitched for the Dodgers. Game one ended in a 1-0 Yankee victory, with a total of only seven hits for both sides in the game. Frustration continued for the Dodgers, who dropped this World Series to the boys from the Bronx in five games. (Courtesy the National Archives.)

The 1950s opened with new possibilities for baseball and America, thanks to Jackie Robinson, Branch Rickey, a supportive Dodger team, and a nation ready for change. The Civil Rights movement had not yet blossomed, but the consciousness of the country had been raised by the revolution in baseball. Resistance was still present, to be sure, but the torch of hope had been lit, and Robinson was its bearer. He had become the focal point in this volatile controversy, and his character proved up to the challenge. In this clearly symbolic, posed photograph, Robinson, with Roy Campanella's son David (left), joins young Larry Solomon (right) to pay tribute to Abraham Lincoln on the Great Emancipator's birthday in 1951. They brought bouquets of flowers on that chilly February day to grace the bronze statue of Lincoln at the Essex County Courthouse in Newark, New Jersey.

Eight
1950–1959

The 1950s were a decade of pennants for the Dodgers. After championship seasons in the Senior Circuit in 1947 and 1949, the nucleus of players for success had been assembled and would be retained into the 1950s. Brooklyn was the dominant National League team, taking flags in 1952, 1953, 1955, and 1956. Their roster would be the envy of almost any team in baseball history, with four future Hall of Famers playing every day—Jackie Robinson, Pee Wee Reese, Roy Campanella, and Duke Snider. In addition, Carl Furillo, Gil Hodges, and Andy Pafko were in the field, with star moundmen Johnny Podres, Don Newcombe, and Carl Erskine. Year in and year out, these fan favorites put up numbers that kept the club at or near the top of the standings. Snider is facing the camera in this early-1950s photograph. The team seems concerned with the game, perhaps at a crucial point in the late innings. Next to Snider is coach Billy Herman, with Podres to his right. Farther down the bench, Campanella leans forward in his catcher's gear.

As this photograph was being taken, the "shot heard round the world" was still reverberating in the Polo Grounds. Moments before, Bobby Thomson had ended the Dodgers' season with his dramatic October 3, 1951 home run. The round tripper set New York City alight, but Brooklyn was plunged into darkness. Jackie Robinson (in the foreground with his back to the camera) is clearly stunned. Ralph Branca, who served up the fatal pitch, is headed quickly toward the camera and the center-field gate. Thomson had just crossed the plate, and the mob scene was just getting started. The crowd was howling with joy and the photographers were snapping away as the Giants reached the 1951 World Series and the Dodgers prepared for winter. Brooklyn had looked the better club, leading the league in runs, hits, doubles, home runs, batting average, and on-base and slugging percentage. It was all for naught after Thomson's celebrated blow.

Slugging Gil Hodges enjoyed his role with the Dodgers. He covered his position gracefully, batted low in the order, and drove in many runs. In 1949, he first hit more than 20 home runs, which he would continue to do through 1959. He hit 370 all told, each one of them for the Bums, with a high of 42 in 1954. He drove in more than 100 runs from 1949 to 1955. He won a Gold Glove three times, was an All-Star eight times, and for a time held the National League record for grand slams (14). When Hodges was going 0 for 21 in the 1952 World Series, Dodger fans said prayers for him. Things improved. Hodges homered regularly in World Series to come, including the game winner in 1956, game one. Hodges moved with the franchise at the end of the decade and won game four of the 1959 World Series with another dramatic four-base hit.

111

Handy Andy Pafko was with winners wherever he played. He became part of the Dodgers greatest outfield ever, occupying left while Duke Snider was in center, and Carl Furillo was in right. He played only two years in Brooklyn but was instrumental in winning the 1952 pennant, driving in 85 runs, with 19 homers.

Duke Snider was jubilant as he crossed the plate after his round-tripper in the sixth game of the 1952 World Series. Snider tied a record at that time, collecting his fourth home run of the World Series. Still, the Bums could not come back from a one-run deficit, and the next day lost the World Series in another squeaker, by a 4-2 score.

That Snider held other World Series records is not too surprising, since he was in six of them. He hit more World Series home runs than anyone else (11) and hit four home runs in a World Series twice, again in 1955. Snider was an all-around good athlete, covering center field with quickness and grace and possessing a strong throwing arm. However, he won most of his honors with his bat.

Junior Gilliam played a full rookie year as the Dodgers' second baseman in 1953. The season was followed by the World Series. In this stop-and-start action shot during game three, Gilliam has knocked down a hot grounder off the bat of Phil Rizzuto. He and shortstop Pee Wee Reese grappled to find the handle before Billy Martin got to second. Martin was safe, but the Dodgers won this one 3-2.

It was a no-hitter that gathered this happy postgame group for photographs in the clubhouse. Carl Erskine, the ace of the Bums' pitching staff, accomplished the feat on June 19, 1952. Dodgers owner Walter O'Malley, who was later castigated for moving the team to Los Angeles, is shown giving a $500 check to Erskine in recognition of his feat.

Joe Black started his baseball career in the Negro League, pitching for the Baltimore Elite Giants, for whom he won 10, 11, and 8 games in 1948, 1949, and 1950, respectively. He worked two years in the minors before winning rookie of the year honors for the Dodgers in 1952, primarily as a reliever. In this view, a 28-year-old Black displays his fastball grip to a couple of visiting Little Leaguers.

They came from Coney Island, Flatbush, Bay Ridge, Prospect Park, Canarsie, Sheepshead Bay, Bushwick, Greenpoint, New Lots, Kensington, Fort Hamilton, New Utrecht, Crown Heights, and everywhere else in Kings County. They assembled behind police barricades to await the opening of the ticket windows. This photograph was taken an hour before game one of the 1952 World Series started. The line for tickets to the bleachers is boisterous and huge. Fans wave their hands, their newspapers, their hats, and their pennants to cheer their boys on, hoping to overcome the hated Yankees. Consecutive World Series defeats had brought an October pessimism to Dodger fans, but there was always hope. These fans were happily rewarded, as game one went to the Bums 4-2, with Joe Black getting the win. Manager Charlie Dressen had converted Black from a reliever to a starting pitcher for the World Series. Black started two more games in the series but lost them both.

Roy Campanella continued the sterling play begun in the 1940s into the next decade. His annual statistics were of All-Star quality, and he was a rock for the Dodger pitching staff. The automobile accident that ended his career after the 1957 season coincided with the team's transfer to the West Coast. As a result, Campy is always associated with Brooklyn. After being confined to a wheelchair, he devoted himself to charitable work in the community.

Whenever Dodger players are recalled, Ralph Branca's name comes up. Brooklyn fans remember him most for giving up Bobby Thomson's home run that decided the 1951 playoffs. There were bright spots, however. In 1947, at age 21, Branca won 21 games. He was also the winner of the 1947 World Series game saved by Al Gionfriddo's catch. Still, the Thomson home run would be forever attached to the Branca legacy.

Carl "Oisk" Erskine pitched valiantly for the Dodgers for 12 years. Two of those years were in Los Angeles, after which Erskine retired with a 122-78 lifetime record and a respectable .610 winning percentage. He threw two no-hitters, participated in the 1954 All-Star game, and struck out 14 men in a 1953 World Series contest, setting a record that lasted until 1967. He won 20 games only once, but in that 1953 season, he led the league in winning percentage at .769. The fans loved him, as this photograph clearly shows. They are celebrating his 1952 no-hitter against the Cubs, which they have just witnessed. It is hard to tell who is happiest. Erskine, aided by an errorless fielding performance behind him, retired the last 19 Chicago batters while recording only one strikeout in the entire contest.

The 1955 Dodgers, pictured here, were the team Dodger fans had been waiting for. They were always good enough to win the National League but could never get by the Yankees to be world champions. The 1947, 1949, 1952, and 1953 seasons had all been pennant-winning years; each time, they faced their Bronx counterparts in the World Series. It was tiresome and sickening for the Bums, but 1955 was different. The World Series was still a battle, going seven games.

The Dodger batting order against the Yankees was Junior Gilliam at second, Pee Wee Reese at short, Duke Snider in center field, Roy Campanella catching, Carl Furillo in right field, Gil Hodges at first, Jackie Robinson at third, and Sandy Amoros in left field, followed by the pitcher. The chemistry was right and, finally, the Bums ruled the baseball world.

Many exciting moments accompany any World Series, but 1955 was special. Jackie Robinson was 36 years old that year, but he had not lost his quickness or daring. A sequence camera, the ancestor of the motor drive, was employed to get this series of photographs of Robinson's steal of home in the eighth inning of game one. Yogi Berra was taking the throw (or actually the pitch) from Whitey Ford. Frank Kellert, Dodger pinch hitter, got out of the way and watched umpire Bill Summers call Robinson safe. The bold move was not quite enough though, as the Yankees pulled the game out 6-5 to take a 1-0 lead in the World Series. The start was once again dismal for the Dodger faithful, and things became worse when they lost the second game 4-2. In game three, however, came the turnaround that would lead to a victory in seven.

Johnny Podres, raised in upstate New York, was the left-handed anchor of the pitching staff in the 1955 World Series. He had an unimpressive record of 9-10 during the regular season, but Dodger manager Walt Alston had faith in the southpaw. He beat the Pinstripers in game three and was beatified in Brooklyn after going all the way in game seven, shutting out the opposition 2-0 to win all the marbles.

Jackie Robinson could smell victory. He was all over the place during the 1955 World Series, making things happen. In game five, at Ebbets Field, Robinson is seen racing back to second base as an errant throw is on its way to Yankee shortstop Jerry Coleman. The ball went into left, but Robinson held at second. Jackie did not score, but the Dodgers did win this one 5-3.

Whenever the 1955 World Series is mentioned, Sandy Amoros's circus catch is sure to come up. Like the Robinson steal of home, this sequence captures the action in stages. At full speed, Amoros approached the left-field fence after the drive off Yogi Berra's bat in the sixth inning of game seven. The grab is credited with saving the World Series for the Dodgers, since two men were on base at the time. Amoros quickly heaved the ball back in to the infield, in time to double up Gil McDougald, who could not get back to first. Podres held the Yanks the rest of the way, and the Dodgers were winners. Amoros, a native of Cuba, played mainly with the Dodgers from 1952 to 1957. He was a journeyman outfielder, who made a play when it most counted. As a result, his name is a happy part of baseball history.

Before the start of every World Series, obligatory photographs are taken of the opposing starting pitchers and managers. Casey Stengel and Walt Alston oblige in this 1956 ceremonial shot before the start of combat. This was the eighth Fall Classic for Stengel and the second for Alston. The Dodger skipper had tasted victory the year before, but Stengel had the last laugh in 1956.

General manager Walter O'Malley had decided that more pitching was needed for the world champions to repeat in 1956. So, on May 15, he bought Sal Maglie from the Cleveland Indians. Maglie had been a nemesis to the Dodgers while pitching for the cross-river Giants for more than six seasons. Maglie went a healthy 13-5, started games one and five in October—winning the first and losing the fifth but pitching very well in both.

Don Newcombe, the Dodgers' huge right-handed starter, took the mound for games two and seven of the 1956 World Series against the Yankees. He had been 20-5 in the 1955 season, besting all other National League pitchers with an .800 winning percentage. And, in 1956, he carried a 27-7 record into postseason play. The Dodgers won game two, but Newcombe did not get the decision. In game seven, at home, we see the first pitch of the game being thrown by Newcombe. Hank Bauer, Yankee right fielder, awaited the pitch, which he promptly whacked into left field for a single. Newcombe went only three innings in this one, coming out the game's loser. The final score was a disturbing 9-0. The Dodgers would not be in another World Series in the borough, playing next in 1959 as representatives of Los Angeles.

Among Dodger fans were many famous screwballs. The loudest and perhaps most notable was the Sym-Phony, organized by Shorty Laurice, wearing the "Our Bums" top hat in this picture. Claiming to be the worst band in the world, these were not musicians but a group of dedicated noisemakers determined to bring victory to Ebbets Field with their cheerful commotion.

After Brooklyn's Musicians Union had the Sym-Phony shut down for playing publicly without a contract, the Dodger brass decided to remedy the ridiculous situation. They offered free admission to any fan who would bring an instrument to the ballpark for Music Appreciation Night. Here, we see 11-year-old Jimmy Lupi of Hoyt Street, who carries his sousaphone past a puzzled usher.

Carl Furillo roamed right field for Brooklyn from 1946 to 1957. His finest year was 1953, when his .344 average won a batting championship, and his ninth-inning home run tied up game six of the World Series. He played 15 years in a Dodger uniform, recording 1,910 total hits, 192 home runs, and a lifetime batting average of .299.

The old and the new posed at the start of the 1957 season, the last for the Dodgers in Brooklyn. Before the opener at Ebbets Field, young Don Drysdale, who made his name later in Los Angeles, shows off his Harold C. Burr Award for being the team's top rookie in 1956. Veteran Don Newcombe (right) displays two 1956 prizes. He had won both the Cy Young Award and the MVP award for the National League.

It would appear from this 1957 action shot that the Dodgers were not going to leave Brooklyn peacefully. The Bums had not been successful by backing down from confrontations, and this day in June was no different. They were still in the pennant race when the Milwaukee Braves came to town. Don Drysdale, never shy about pitching inside, had provoked hot-headed Johnny Logan (No. 23 for the Braves), who is shown preparing to unload a punch at manager Walt Alston (No. 24 for the Dodgers). Meanwhile, Pee Wee Reese (center rear) tries to keep Eddie Mathews away from Drysdale (on the ground behind Logan). The Braves first-base coach (right) restrains another Dodger. Logan received a league fine of $100, and Reese received one for $40. No one recorded who won this fight, but the Braves went on to win the pennant by 8 games over the Cardinals and 11 over the Dodgers.

Anguished protests and the startled disbelief of adoring fans were not enough to keep the Dodgers in Brooklyn. Greed, as embodied in owner Walter O'Malley, overcame all sentiment for letting the Bums stay—at least, the fans in New York saw it that way. Long before he ever thought of owning a ball club, he abandoned the loyalty, tradition, and community spirit that had distinguished the franchise in Brooklyn. The city had a hole in its soul, thanks to O'Malley, and Brooklynites still have not forgotten. The betrayal was made worse since the Dodgers had been world champions just two years before, and the fans believed they were truly a part of that victory. Few continued to follow the team in Los Angeles, both as a protest and recognition that the Dodgers were no longer theirs. The move to California by both the Giants and Dodgers will always be remembered as a sad time for traditionalists in baseball history. Gone in a flash were two venerable franchises, leaving a sour taste in the mouths of New York fans but also leaving behind wonderful memories.